SEASONS

WHAT I SEE IN FALL

by Danielle J. Jacks

TABLE OF CONTENTS

tadpole books

WORDS TO KNOW

apples

coats

costumes

leaves

pumpkins

school bus

WHAT I SEE IN FALL

It is fall!

It gets colder.

We wear coats.

Leaves fall.

We rake.

Apples grow.

I eat one. Yum!

I see a school bus.

We go to school!

I see pumpkins.

We carve them!

I see costumes.

Trick or treat!

LET'S REVIEW!

What are these kids doing in fall?

INDEX